BENITO MUSSOLINI

FASCIST ITALIAN DICTATOR

SPECIAL LIVES IN HISTORY THAT BECOME

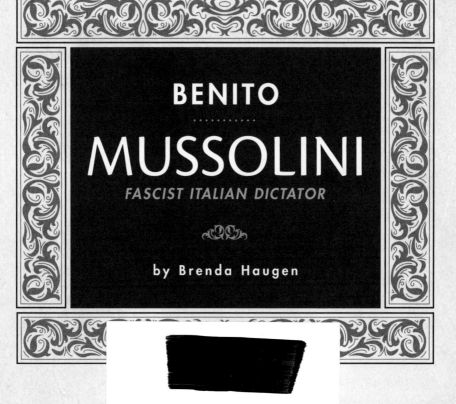

BENITO
MUSSOLINI
FASCIST ITALIAN DICTATOR

by Brenda Haugen

Content Adviser: Ruth Ben-Ghiat,
Professor of Italian Studies and History,
New York University

Reading Adviser: Rosemary G. Palmer, Ph.D.,
Department of Literacy, College of Education,
Boise State University

Compass Point Books ✦ Minneapolis, Minnesota

Compass Point Books
3109 West 50th Street, #115
Minneapolis, MN 55410

Visit Compass Point Books on the Internet at *www.compasspointbooks.com*
or e-mail your request to *custserv@compasspointbooks.com*

Editor: Anthony Wacholtz
Page Production: Noumenon Creative
Photo Researcher: Eric Gohl
Cartographer: XNR Productions, Inc.
Library Consultant: Kathleen Baxter

Art Director: Jaime Martens
Creative Director: Keith Griffin
Editorial Director: Carol Jones
Managing Editor: Catherine Neitge

*To my dear friend Lynne Lundberg and her parents for being my fans all
my life. BLH*

Library of Congress Cataloging-in-Publication Data
Haugen, Brenda
  Benito Mussolini : Fascist Italian Dictator / by Brenda Haugen.
      p. cm.—(Signature lives)
  Includes bibliographical references and index.
  ISBN-13: 978-0-7565-1892-9 (library binding)
  ISBN-10: 0-7565-1892-X (library binding)
  ISBN-13: 978-0-7565-1988-9 (paperback)
  ISBN-10: 0-7565-1988-8 (paperback)
  1. Mussolini, Benito, 1883–1945—Juvenile literature. 2. Heads of
state—Italy—Biography—Juvenile literature. 3. Italy—Politics and gov-
ernment—1914–1945—Juvenile literature. 4. Fascism—Italy—History—
20th century—Juvenile literature. I. Title. II. Series.
  DG575.M8H35 2007
  945.091092—dc22   2006027069
  [B]

MODERN WORLD

From 1900 to the present day, humanity and the world have undergone major changes. New political ideas resulted in worldwide wars. Fascism and communism divided some countries, and democracy brought others together. Drastic shifts in theories and practice tested the standards of personal freedoms and religious conventions as well as science, technology, and industry. These changes have created a need for world policies and an understanding of international relations. The new mind-set of the modern world includes a focus on humanitarianism and the belief that a global economy has made the world a more connected place.

Benito Mussolini

Table of Contents

1 DEATH OF A DICTATOR

❧⤫❧

Italians either loved or hated Benito Mussolini. A brutal dictator who did not care for those he ruled, Mussolini was executed by his own citizens on April 28, 1945. Dying alongside him was one of many women who loved him. Whether taken by his power or his charm, Claretta Petacci was unable to face the prospect of life without him. She died at his side.

The bodies of Mussolini, Petacci, and 12 disgraced Italian leaders who had also been executed were piled onto a truck in the northern Italian village of Dongo and driven to Milan, Italy. There, in the town square, Mussolini's lifeless corpse hung upside down next to the others to be abused by the crowd that had gathered. The angry mob spat and cursed as it beat Mussolini's dead body. For years, Mussolini had ruled

Benito Mussolini was the dictator of Italy from 1922 to 1943.

The bodies of Mussolini, Petacci, and other Italian leaders were hung by their feet as a public spectacle.

Italy with fear and violence. Now Italy's citizens were getting their revenge.

Eventually, the crowd was turned away, and Mussolini's body was untied. He was buried in an unmarked grave in a Milan cemetery. In 1957, his

body was moved to his family's mausoleum in the San Cassiano cemetery in Predappio, Italy.

On April 25, 1945, just days before his death, Mussolini had fled from Milan. World War II was drawing to an end, and Mussolini knew he was in trouble. He did not want to be captured by the Allies, his foes in the war. Mussolini knew his countrymen would be of no help. They hated him for all the pain and suffering he had forced upon them, particularly during the war.

On April 27, Mussolini joined a group of German soldiers hoping to find safety in Switzerland. But Mussolini would never make it across the border. The German troops were allowed to continue on their journey, but Italian forces opposed to the dictator discovered him among the group. They held him as a prisoner before executing him.

Mussolini's death was no more violent than his life. He had worked his way into power from very humble beginnings. A troubled youth, Mussolini struggled early in his life. He failed as a schoolteacher, but he gained attention as a political writer. However, he never stood firm on any ideas. He changed his opinions and beliefs as it suited him. Throughout his life, he would change from one political platform to another, depending on his audience and on whether he believed the change would bring him more power. In 1922, he gained the high office he wanted, becoming

*An American
soldier gazed
at a bullet-
riddled poster
of Mussolini
in Italy.*

the youngest prime minister in Italian history.

To some Italians, Mussolini seemed to be a savior. They looked to him and his government to save them from poverty and despair. To others, he

An American soldier gazed at a bullet-riddled poster of Mussolini in Italy.

was just the best choice in an era that did not seem to hold many promising options. Mussolini found Italians were willing to accept him not just as the prime minister but as a dictator. In exchange for the promise of order, prosperity, and the return of national pride, people were willing to give up some of their personal freedoms.

But after 20 years with Mussolini as their leader, Italians found themselves no better off than they had been before. As their country was overrun by foreign troops near the end of World War II, Italians proved they had finally had enough of Mussolini and his tyranny. A cruel leader who used intimidation, imprisonment, and even murder to hold on to power, Mussolini himself would meet a grisly end at the hands of his own citizens. ✒

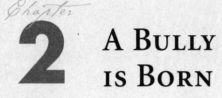

2 A BULLY IS BORN

❦

On July 29, 1883, Benito Mussolini entered the world. He was the first child born to Alessandro and Rosa Mussolini. It was not a happy family. Alessandro was an alcoholic who had trouble keeping a job. He chose to name his son Benito Amilcare Andrea Mussolini, after three of his radical revolutionary heroes: Benito Juárez, Amilcare Cipriani, and Andrea Costa.

Before his marriage to Rosa, Alessandro had a troubled history. Because of his beliefs, which included a violent overthrow of the government, he often found himself on the wrong side of the law. In October 1878, Alessandro was placed under house arrest after officials suspected he was taking part in revolutionary activities. He was allowed to work but could not leave Verano di

Costa, the town in northeast Italy where he lived. He also was required to report to the police every Sunday morning.

Wanting to avoid prison, Alessandro followed the rules of his arrest. He soon discovered another reason to stay out of trouble. He had fallen in love with a sweet schoolteacher named Rosa Maltoni. Rosa's father did not approve of the match at all. Rosa was raised as a Catholic, and Alessandro did not believe in God and hated the Catholic Church. However, his love for Rosa was stronger than his hatred of religion. He agreed to a church wedding and married Rosa on January 25, 1882.

Appearing as a respectable married man, Alessandro appealed to officials to be released from his house arrest, and in October 1882, the sentence was lifted. But the next year, when he named his son after his three favorite revolutionaries, Alessandro proved marriage really had not changed him.

Despite what she may have thought about her husband's beliefs, Rosa held her family together. In 1885, Benito was joined

Benito Juárez was a revolutionary who served two terms as president of Mexico in the mid-1800s. Amilcare Cipriani fought by the side of Italian revolutionary Giuseppe Garibaldi and attempted to free Rome from France in 1862. Though Cipriani was exiled for his actions, he returned to Italy in 1880 as a hero. Andrea Costa was an anarchist, a person who believes in the overthrow of government. He planned a failed revolution in Bologna, Italy, in the late 1800s.

by a brother, Arnaldo. In 1888, the birth of Benito's sister, Edvige, completed the family. Along with raising her children, Rosa worked as a teacher. The community provided a small three-room home for the schoolmistress, and it was here the Mussolinis lived. The family occupied two rooms, and the third room served as the classroom where Rosa taught school.

When he was old enough, Benito began helping his father at the forge where he worked as a blacksmith. Alessandro used the time to teach Benito about socialism and the revolutionary ideas of Karl Marx and others he admired. Alessandro also continued to drink a great deal and even cheated on his wife.

Alessandro was careless with the money he earned. However, the family survived because they lived frugally. The family's meals usually consisted of black bread and soup. On Sundays, the family splurged and ate meat. Though the Mussolini family did not have much money, their home did include a large number of books, and Benito loved to read.

Benito was a moody child. As a boy, he rarely laughed and made no friends. This would not change as he grew older. He would rather stay alone and read

Alessandro Mussolini believed the wealth in Italy should be shared more fairly.

Rosa Mussolini helped support her family by teaching as a schoolmistress.

than spend time with others. But he adored his mother, who always told him he was capable of great things. Benito wrote in his 1928 autobiography:

My greatest love was for my mother. She was so quiet, so tender, and yet so strong. ... My mother not only reared us but she taught primary school. I often thought, even in my earliest appreciation of human beings, of how faithful and patient her work was. To displease her was my one fear.

A violent bully, Benito liked to pick fights with other children. "More than once I came back home with my head bleeding from a blow with a stone," he remembered. "But I knew how to defend myself." Knowing this would disappoint his mother, Benito hid his cuts and bruises from her.

At age 9, Benito was sent to a boarding school run by priests. His mother hoped that someday he would become a priest, too. However, he hated the school and saw being sent there as a punishment. Discipline by the priests was harsh. It included beatings as well as forcing students to stay in a room alone. The harsh

A letter from the school principal detailed Benito's disruptive behavior, which led to a 10-day suspension.

punishments made Benito more defiant and angry. In 1893, he stabbed a fellow student and was expelled.

A second boarding school proved more to Benito's liking. At his first boarding school, Benito sometimes had to be dragged to Mass, the Catholic Church service. Church attendance at his new school was not required, which made him happy. The new school also proved to be a kinder place that served better food and was close enough to his family that he could go home on the weekends. Though he still made no effort to make friends, Benito became more involved in school. He even played trombone in the school band. He loved music and later taught himself to play the violin. As an adult, he would play the violin to relax.

Playing the violin was a hobby Mussolini continued throughout his adulthood.

But these positive changes in Benito's life did not keep him out of trouble. He was asked to leave

the school after a fight but was able to stay when the incident blew over. On two other occasions, however, he was suspended and sent home for 10 days. Again, one of the incidents involved stabbing another student.

During his last two years at the school, Benito began to date. He sometimes chose older women and did not care if they were married. If anyone criticized his choices, he used violence to silence them.

A smart student, Benito earned average grades. He made a positive impact at school, however, when he was chosen to give his first speech. In January 1901, the school honored Italian composer Giuseppe Verdi, who had recently died. Benito was excited to speak in Verdi's honor and discovered he was good at it. His teachers praised him for his efforts.

Later that year, Benito graduated with a certificate that would allow him to teach school, but he also wanted to be a writer. Soon he would get his opportunity to both teach and write. ❧

Born in 1813 near Parma, Italy, Giuseppe Verdi composed 26 operas as well as many other musical compositions during his lifetime. A strong patriot, Verdi became a symbol of Italy's fight for independence from Austria in the mid-1800s. Some Austrian officials believed he used his operas to stir Italian national pride and a thirst for independence. After Verdi's death, a period of national mourning followed in Italy.

3 TEACHER AND JOURNALIST

❧⟨✦⟩❧

As an adult, Benito Mussolini developed some of his father's bad habits, as well as a few of his own. He began drinking heavily and gambling. He also peppered his language with swearing.

After graduation, Mussolini avoided getting a job until he had no money left at all. He tried to get some of his poetry published, but with no success. So in early 1902, he took a position as a substitute teacher at an elementary school in the small town of Gualtieri, in northern Italy.

Mussolini was not very excited about being a teacher. When he found out how difficult a job it was, he liked it even less. As a teacher, he discovered his bad habits made him unpopular with his students' parents—and his students did not like him either.

In his spare time, Mussolini began writing articles for socialist magazines. He joined the local socialist group and quickly became the organization's secretary.

When Mussolini's teaching job ended in June, the school did not offer him a permanent position, but he did not care. He decided to go to neighboring Switzerland instead, possibly to avoid military service.

Mussolini lied to his mother and said a job awaited him there. She gave her son a whole month's salary so he could buy a train ticket. Giving up the money at that time was a particular hardship because his father, Alessandro, had been arrested. He was charged with starting a riot and ignoring election laws by assaulting a voting clerk and throwing the ballots he found into the wind. Though he was found not guilty, Alessandro spent six months in jail before going to trial.

When he arrived in Switzerland, Mussolini merely wandered around. He hated hard work and rarely stayed at a job for long. He begged and stole to survive. Considering himself to be better than the poor and homeless, he often slept in the

Switzerland is a land-locked country in western Europe. The country holds a long tradition of neutrality. Though it boasts no formal army, Swiss men still go through military training and can be called to service at any time. However, since the 1500s, Switzerland has stayed out of conflict in Europe, even during World War I and World War II.

street rather than in homeless shelters.

He continued trying to make a living as a writer. He submitted poems and articles to socialist magazines.

Mussolini believed poor people would continue to suffer under Italy's government. He thought the only way to make life fairer for all Italians would be to overthrow the current government and build a new, socialist one. A common way for workers to gain better wages and working conditions was by striking, refusing to work until their conditions were

Strikers threw chairs and overturned tables in a cafe in Misian, Italy.

met. Mussolini believed strikes were a waste of time. He encouraged violence and terrorism to change the entire system of government.

Some socialists were more patient. They wanted to gain power by earning seats in parliament. Because elected socialists would have to work with other political parties in parliament, Mussolini believed the only way to truly gain power was to destroy parliament, not join it. He excited young socialists who were impatient for change. In time, more and more people became interested in what Mussolini had to say.

His call for the violent overthrow of the govern-

ment also caught the attention of the police. On June 18, 1903, Mussolini was arrested in Berne, Switzerland, for his talk of revolution. Officials there feared he would inspire workers to commit violence.

After spending nearly two weeks in jail, Mussolini was sent back to Italy. Not wanting to remain there and face military service for a government he did not support, Mussolini sneaked back into Switzerland. In Lausanne on March 18, 1904, Mussolini met Angelica Balabanoff. Though she grew up living a life of privilege, Balabanoff rebelled against her family and became a socialist. Although she saw Mussolini as an unclean man with uncombed hair and wrinkled clothes, she also thought he was smart. With Balabanoff's help, Mussolini began to rise in importance among the socialists. In time, he became a member of the Italian Socialist Party's Central Committee.

In late 1904, the Italian government declared a general amnesty for those who avoided military service. This meant Mussolini could return to his homeland without being arrested, but he would still be required to fulfill his military duty. He discovered that his mother had become ill with meningitis, so he decided to return to Italy. When Mussolini arrived at home, he taught his mother's classes to give her a break before joining his regiment in January.

Not long after joining his fellow soldiers, Mussolini learned his mother's health had grown worse. In February, she was near death. He was allowed to go home and arrived shortly before Rosa died on February 19, 1905. She was 46 years old.

Mussolini finished his required 21-month stint in the army in September 1906. He decided to teach again, this time in the small town of Tolmezzo, Italy. Although he tried bribing them with treats, he was unable to keep his students under control. The children disliked him and showed him no respect, nicknaming him the "Tyrant."

In his free time, Mussolini continued to gamble and drink, and he could not keep his bad habits a secret in the small town. When the time came for the school to renew his teaching contract, the parents of Tolmezzo let the contract expire. Mussolini again found himself without a job.

In early 1907, he drew the attention of police when he started spewing hatred toward Catholics in his socialist speeches. He quickly realized the police were keeping him under constant watch.

After his mother's death, Mussolini's father was forced to give up the cottage in which they had lived. His father moved to Forli, and Mussolini decided to join him.

Hoping he would do better teaching secondary school students rather than elementary children, Mussolini took foreign language classes in order to qualify to work with the older students. He took exams in French and German but only qualified to teach French; he failed the German exam.

While staying in Forli, Mussolini started dating Rachele Guidi, a former student of his mother's. Now 16, Rachele was working as a live-in maid for a wealthy family in Forli. Her widowed mother, Anna, worked for Alessandro Mussolini as his live-in housekeeper. Mussolini became reacquainted with Rachele when she came to visit her mother. Though he had publicly embarrassed and sometimes even struck the women he dated, Mussolini treated Rachele relatively well.

Rachele Guidi (1890–1979)

In March 1908, he took a teaching position in Oneglia on the Italian Riviera. He also began writing and editing a socialist newspaper. But Mussolini proved to be no better at teaching there than he had been anywhere else. Within four months, he was fired. He moved back to Forli to live with his father, and he continued his relationship with Rachele. ❧

4 TROUBLE WITH THE LAW

❦

On July 13, 1908, socialists in the parish of Predappio organized a rally to support a group of workers who went on strike. The workers were protesting against conditions at a local factory and against the new employees, known as scabs, who had been hired to replace them. Armed troops broke up the rally, but the situation remained tense. Five days later, Mussolini tested the tension by threatening the factory manager when he saw him on the street.

The factory owner reported the incident to police, and Mussolini was arrested. Found guilty of threatening to harm the man, Mussolini was sentenced to three months in prison. However, he appealed the decision and was released from jail at the end of July while the case was reviewed. In

November, the appeals court said it agreed with the conviction but reduced Mussolini's sentence to the time he had already served in jail.

The time spent behind bars did not stop Mussolini from getting into trouble. On February 6, 1909, he moved to Trent, Italy, to edit a weekly socialist newspaper. He angered Catholics by attacking the morals of area priests. Charged twice with libel, Mussolini paid a fine in the first case and faced jail again for the second incident. However, upon appeal, he escaped any jail time.

While Mussolini publicly questioned the morals of priests, he did not worry about his own character. When he left Forli for Trent, he had promised Rachele that in time he would marry her. He also gave his word that he would write to her, but he never did. Instead, he started affairs with at least two women— Ida Dalser and a married woman named Fernanda Oss Facchinelli. As a result of their affair, Facchinelli gave birth to Mussolini's son. However, the child died as an infant. Not long after the baby's death, Facchinelli died of tuberculosis.

In August 1909, Mussolini was arrested two more times and jailed for abusing the freedom of the press for his continued libelous attacks. No longer welcome in Trent, he returned to live with his father in Forli.

Benito and Rachele eventually decided to live together. Neither of their parents were happy that their children were living together without being married. Mussolini convinced them to change their minds by going to his father's house and issuing a threat. Armed with a loaded gun, Mussolini said he would kill himself and Rachele if Alessandro and Anna did not give the couple their blessing. On January 17, 1910, Benito and Rachele began their life together in their own home. Alessandro did not live much longer, though; he died on November 17, 1910, at the age of 56.

Meanwhile, Mussolini worked in Forli as a socialist newspaper editor. *La Lotta di Classe* (The Class Struggle) was first published January 9, 1910. Right away, Mussolini tried to stir up trouble by calling for a revolution. He wanted to see a fight between the wealthy and the poor. He wrote articles saying

The Italian Socialist Party boasted many leaders in 1908. Intrigued by the party's beliefs and growing popularity, Mussolini spread the socialist viewpoint in La Lotta di Classe.

socialists should forget about working for change within the present system of government. He wanted the government destroyed, but he offered no details on rebuilding the country after such a revolution.

In 1911, France and Britain each claimed parts of Africa, and Italy wanted a piece of the continent as well. Italy found a reason to threaten Turkey, which ruled Libya, a country in northern Africa. Italy demanded that its own troops be allowed into Libya to protect Italian citizens living there. When Turkey refused to bow to this demand, the Italo-Turkish War erupted. The war lasted until late 1912, when Turkey admitted defeat and turned Libya over to Italian control. Italy proved to be a cruel ruler. It used concentration camps to punish those who dared fight against its rule.

In 1912, Mussolini spoke out against the Italian government's war with Turkish-held provinces that are known today as Libya. During a September 24 town meeting, he advocated blowing up Italian train tracks to hamper the war effort. Three weeks later, he was arrested on charges of inciting violence. Mussolini felt no regret. At the trial, he told the judge:

> *If you find me not guilty, I will be pleased; if you find me guilty, I will be honored.*

Mussolini was found guilty and sentenced to a year in prison. After appealing the decision, his prison time was reduced to 5½ months. Mussolini did not waste the time behind bars. He used it to write his autobiography.

Just two days after his release

from prison, Mussolini expressed disgust over the actions of some of the socialist members of Italy's parliament. These socialists had congratulated Italy's monarch, King Victor Emmanuel III, on surviving a recent attempt on his life. Mussolini believed the king's death would be a good thing for Italy. He thought if the king were assassinated, Italians might take the opportunity to form a new government. In an article in Forli's socialist newspaper, Mussolini wrote that the socialists who had congratulated the king should be thrown out of the party.

King Victor Emmanuel III (1869–1947)

He repeated this belief at the July 1912 Socialist Party meeting. Others agreed with him, which led to a division in the party. Many of the party's top leaders were kicked out of the organization. In addition, the party chose a new National Executive Committee to lead them. Mussolini was among those chosen to serve on the committee. This new position of leadership brought Mussolini international attention. ❧

5 *Avanti!*

With his new status in the Socialist Party, Mussolini was asked to become the editor of *Avanti!*—meaning "Forward!"—the party's national daily newspaper. Party leaders would not be disappointed. Within a year, the circulation of the newspaper nearly doubled to 60,000.

Though the newspaper job paid a modest salary, Mussolini insisted his wages be cut in half to appear selfless. Although he lived frugally and believed he did not need a larger paycheck, he was supporting two households. Mussolini had moved to Milan to start his new job at the newspaper, and he also sent money to Rachele, who remained in Forli with their 2-year-old daughter, Edda.

Mussolini hired Angelica Balabanoff as his

As editor of Avanti!, *Mussolini showcased socialist revolutionary Amilcare Cipriani—one of the men he was named after—on the January 16, 1914, front page.*

assistant editor. He knew she was smart and knew more about politics than he did. He also liked having her around for another reason. Without Rachele's knowledge, he was having an affair with Balabanoff.

Mussolini also had rekindled his love affair with Ida Dalser. Believing she was in love with him, Dalser had moved to Milan to be closer to him and opened a beauty shop. Throughout his life, Mussolini found many women were attracted to him. Some liked being with a man who held power. He also could be very charming when he wanted to be.

In January 1913, riots erupted in central Italy. Farmworkers were angry with the government, which had failed to keep its promise of providing a sanitation system for them. Troops were sent to quiet the situation, but bloodshed quickly put an end to any hope of a peaceful solution. Seven farmers were killed and even more were injured in skirmishes with the soldiers. News of the violence spread and so did the rioting.

Mussolini was delighted. He published articles in *Avanti!* that would ensure the anger did not die down. He blamed the country's royal family for the situation and encouraged citizens to respond with more violence. The tension grew after a worker named Augusto Massetti shot an army officer who had nothing to do with the farmers' deaths. A court found Massetti insane and threw him into an asylum. To

Italian farmers went on strike after the government failed to provide an adequate sanitation system.

show their support for Massetti, trade unions across the country called for a strike on June 7, 1914.

Though he had shown contempt for strikes in the past, Mussolini supported this one. He believed the strike would add to growing discontent with the country's government. Mussolini praised the strike in articles he wrote for his newspaper. The Socialist Party also sided with the workers. However, when the strike turned violent, the party called for an end to it. Though Mussolini liked violence and would have liked to see the strike go on, he followed the beliefs of his party. In the June 12 issue of *Avanti!*, he called the strike a success and urged people to go back to work.

International events quickly took Italy's attention away from its problems at home. Franz Ferdinand, archduke of Austria-Hungary, was visiting Sarajevo, the capital of Bosnia-Herzegovina, with his wife, Duchess Sophie. A Serbian terrorist named Gavrilo Princip assassinated the couple on June 28.

Austria-Hungary's government believed the Serbian government was behind the murders. It responded by declaring war on Serbia, marking the start of World War I. Mussolini spoke out against the war. He thought it was being fought by countries hoping to gain territory, which he opposed. Serbia had won its independence from Austria-Hungary before the assassinations, and Mussolini believed Austria-Hungary was using the murders as an excuse to overrun Serbia again.

Two days after the war was declared, Russia entered the war on Serbia's side. On August 1, Germany

As heir to the Austro-Hungarian throne, Franz Ferdinand defied convention and married his true love, a low-ranking countess named Sophie Chotek, on July 1, 1900. Ferdinand's uncle, Emperor Franz Josef of Austria, was so disappointed by the union, he refused to attend the ceremony. The marriage was only allowed after Ferdinand and Sophie agreed that Sophie would not be given royal status. In addition, they also forfeited any claims to the throne that their future children might have.

joined the fight, siding with Austria-Hungary. World War I was under way.

While other countries joined the fray, Mussolini urged Italy to remain neutral. However, he would soon change his mind. Some Italian socialists began siding with the Allied powers, which included Great Britain, Russia, and France. This group of Italians would come to be known as the country's first fascists. Later, Mussolini would say he formed the Fascist Party to pressure the Italian government to enter World War I. In reality, the group formed in October, and Mussolini did not join it until December.

The Los Angeles Times *announced Germany's invasion of France on August 3, 1914.*

Despite the desire of some to support the Allies, the socialists' National Executive Committee voted in the fall to remain neutral. Mussolini insisted an emergency party meeting be held to examine the socialists' position on the war. However, the National Executive Committee refused to call for such a meeting. An angry Mussolini resigned his position at

Avanti! Many in the party were shocked at his change of heart regarding the war. Less than two weeks later, Socialist Party members voted to kick Mussolini out of their organization.

Mussolini did not care, though. He would change his mind whenever he thought the change might bring him more power and influence. He also discovered his readers were not bothered by his changing opinions. They liked his writing style. He took extreme positions whenever possible, which attracted attention and drew even more readers.

Since Mussolini had dreamed of running his own newspaper, he now took the time to make it a reality. Though it was called *The People of Italy*, his newspaper reflected his own ideas, not those of everyday citizens.

Mussolini once said the war was a plot by powerful countries to take over weaker nations. Now he called the war a battle to free the oppressed. By taking the Allies' side in the war, Mussolini found new resources available to him. Allied supporters helped fund his newspaper. He also received money from Italian businessmen who had more to gain if Italy entered the war. Even the Italian government helped fund his newspaper. For years, Mussolini had called for the violent overthrow of the government. Now, however, he had no problem taking money from the administration he once had said he hated. ✍

6 WORLD WAR I

❦❧

Mussolini continued to speak out about his desire that Italy join the war. In secret, the Italian government was planning just that. However, it was waiting to see which side—the Allies or the Central Powers—would offer it the best deal for joining.

On April 26, 1915, Italy signed the Treaty of London with the Allies—France, Russia, and Great Britain. The treaty offered Italy more territory for entering the war than the Central Powers could. So on May 24, Italy entered the fight on the Allies' side and declared war on Austria-Hungary. Unaware of the secret treaty, Mussolini took credit for getting the Italian government to enter the war on the side of the Allies. He said his threats of civil war if Italy did not attack Austria-Hungary moved the government

France and Belgium amassed their cavalry at the beginning of World War I.

to action, and many people believed him.

From the start, World War I proved disastrous for Italy. It suffered great losses while gaining nothing. Yet Mussolini was happy. His country was at war, and he got his chance to prove his patriotism.

On August 31, 1915, Mussolini was drafted. He was sent to the front lines on September 17. Soldiers

Mussolini served in the Italian army during World War I.

dealt with horrible conditions. The weather was cold and wet. The trenches in which they fought were riddled with lice. Despite the hardships, Mussolini made the most of his time as a soldier. The other troops liked him, and he quickly rose through the ranks to sergeant.

He continued to write newspaper articles and journal entries even though he remained right in the heat of the fight. On November 11, he received a letter from Ida Dalser in Milan. In it, she said she had given birth to his son, whom she named Benito Albino. Shortly after receiving the letter, Mussolini fell ill with salmonella poisoning. After recovering at a military hospital, he was granted 30 days' leave. Mussolini went back to Forli and married Rachele on December 16, 1915. The following September, their second child, Vittorio, would be born.

Shortly after his wedding to Rachele, Mussolini traveled to Milan where he and Dalser checked into a hotel as husband and wife, even though they were not married. After spending time with her and meeting their son, Mussolini journeyed back to the fighting front.

His visit with Dalser would come back to haunt him. Though Mussolini had been sending her money to support her and their son, she wanted more. In July 1916, she filed court papers asking for alimony, money usually given to a spouse after a couple has divorced. Dalser used the hotel registry as proof that she and Mussolini had been married. Though the court did not believe the marriage claim, it did order him to pay Dalser more money to support her and their son. Though angry, Mussolini followed the court's order. However, he would never have anything to do with Dalser or their son again.

The following spring, he suffered a serious battle injury. Accounts of what happened vary, even according to Mussolini. In his war journal, he wrote that a new piece of equipment overheated and exploded, killing two and wounding him and four others. In his autobiography, he said his injuries resulted from a grenade explosion:

> *The patience and ability of the physicians succeeded in taking out of my body forty-four pieces of the grenade. ... I faced atrocious pain; my suffering was indescribable. ... I had twenty-seven operations in one month; all except two were without anaesthetics.*

While Mussolini probably exaggerated his situation in his autobiography, his injuries were serious, and he was discharged from the army in June. He went back to his newspaper and found plenty to write about. Under poor leadership, the Italian army was dealt one defeat after another. Mussolini wrote

Mussolini suffered serious injuries that ended his time in the army.

that the troops kept facing defeat because the army's generals were secretly against the war. He also blamed Italy's parliament and other leaders for the country's losses in the war—and he was not afraid to say so. Mussolini wanted to rid the country of its parliament and all leaders but one. He believed Italy needed a single leader who could bring the country to glory again, and he wanted to be that leader. 🔊

7 SPREADING A MESSAGE OF FEAR

⟿⟾

Italian families endured tremendous losses during World War I. More than 600,000 soldiers were killed, and more than a million were wounded. Even after the war ended on November 11, 1918, Italy continued to suffer.

Though the Allies won, Italy was left out of most of the spoils, despite the secret treaty it had signed with France, Russia, and Great Britain. Like many Italians, Mussolini felt betrayed. He was angry Italy did not get as much territory as he believed it should have, and in his newspaper, he stirred up anger in others.

Among the disgusted Italians were gangs of war veterans called *arditi*. The violent group opposed socialism and was drawn to fascism. The Fascist Party appealed to veterans with a program supporting

Widespread bombing during World War I had a devastating effect on many Italian cities.

government ownership of national resources. Socialists angered veterans by saying they had been tricked into fighting during World War I by the upper class. They said the veterans were not heroes but merely victims. This offended the veterans and caused hatred toward the socialists.

Socialists also faced opposition from growing numbers of citizens because of their use of strikes to get what they wanted. Italy's economy suffered during and after World War I, and people saw strikes as causing even more economic despair. Socialists became targets for the anger and helplessness some Italians felt. Meanwhile, the fascists believed the government should control labor and industry and put an end to any threat of strikes. They said they would bring order back to the nation.

On April 15, 1919, a group of *arditi* vandalized the *Avanti!* office in Milan. The violence spread, and riots erupted in the streets. Though Mussolini did not participate in the riots, he called this the start of the fascist revolution.

The Treaty of Versailles, written after the end of World War I, gave Italy Trentino and Trieste. However, the secret Treaty of London, signed with Great Britain, Russia, and France in return for Italy's participation in the war, had promised much more. In the Treaty of Versailles, Italy ended up getting exactly what Austria-Hungary had offered for Italy's neutrality, a bitter pill for Italians to swallow after all the suffering and loss of life their countrymen had endured during the war.

Mussolini learned a great deal from the reactions to the Milan riots. He realized the police were more understanding toward the *arditi* than they were toward the socialists. The police were more likely to hit or arrest a socialist than a member of the *arditi*. The fascists could become the dominant party simply by physically beating their opponents.

After the Milan riots, Mussolini started his own branch of *arditi*. With money he earned from his newspaper, he provided his men with weapons and supplies. In time, his newspaper offices looked more like an arsenal than a place of business.

Mussolini (center) used his wealth and influence as the editor of a newspaper to spread fascism.

While working to physically defeat his opponents, Mussolini also decided to run for office. In the past, he had said the government should be violently overthrown. He had argued that change would not come by becoming part of the parliamentary system. Now he was hoping to do just that—change the government by becoming a part of it.

In the November 16, 1919, election, Mussolini was listed as a Fascist Party candidate for parliament. However, he was handily defeated by the Socialist Party candidate, 160,000 to 4,637. Despite growing discontent toward socialism in Italy, the socialists won more seats in the 1919 election than any other party. The fascists did not win any.

Giovanni Giolitti (1842–1928)

But the tide quickly changed. In the summer of 1920, socialists began seizing factories and calling for more strikes in an effort to gain more power for the workers of the country. Italian Prime Minister Giovanni Giolitti brought factory owners and trade union representatives together in Rome to talk things out. Giolitti talked factory owners into paying higher salaries and sharing some of the responsibilities of their businesses' management. However, these changes only caused more problems. Profits declined, leading to a crash of the Italian stock market.

While the lower class had suffered the most since the end of World War I, the stock market crash caused strife among the middle and upper classes as well. People lost their jobs and their savings. More Italians began looking to the Fascist Party to solve their problems.

Mussolini furthered his party's cause by fueling people's fears. Nations around the world worried about the possible spread of Russian communism after World War I. Under communism, all land, houses, factories, and other businesses belonged to the government. Russian people were not free to worship or live their lives as they saw fit. Mussolini stirred up worries that the current Italian government would be powerless to stop the communists if they targeted the country.

Some socialists in Italy believed communism was a good choice for their country. They believed communism would get rid of the social classes. There would no longer be wealthy people and poor people; everyone would be the same. As a result, those afraid of communism now wanted to stamp out socialism, too. In the first months of 1921, *squadristi*—violent

Mussolini excited other Italians with his fascist views during a rally in Rome.

bands similar to the *arditi*—stepped up violence against socialists. Meeting halls and newspaper offices were burned down. Individual socialists were attacked and even killed. Some Italians believed the *squadristi* was doing what the Italian government could not do—keep them safe from communism.

Mussolini probably did not believe communists would really take over Italy. However, he was afraid that socialists might join forces with Italian Prime Minister Giolitti and actually form a parliament that worked. If the government got back on track and improved the lives of citizens, people would grow more happy and content. Mussolini feared this would mean the death of the Fascist Party, which was fueled by the citizens' anger and fear.

To avoid a coalition between Giolitti and the socialists, Mussolini proposed his own coalition with the Giolitti government in 1921. The move angered some fascists who wanted nothing to do with the current government, but Mussolini did not care. It would give him a stronger leadership role, and he believed most fascists would follow him. For his part, Giolitti believed a coalition with the fascists would satisfy the group and make it less dangerous to his government.

Giolitti asked the king to dissolve the parliament and called for a new election. In Milan, Mussolini again ran for a parliament seat. Throughout the country, the election was marred by violence and voter intimidation. In some places, *squadristi* prevented socialists from holding election meetings. Police offered no help to the socialists and sometimes even helped the *squadristi* by lending them vehicles and, in some cases, giving them weapons.

Though Giolitti did not like the violence, he did nothing to stop it. When the votes were counted, the Socialist Party still led the number of seats with 122 deputies elected, but 35 fascists—including Mussolini—were elected to parliament. Though it was far from a majority, the Fascist Party now had a voice in government. Mussolini and other fascists would now take advantage of an Italian law stating parliament members could not be arrested. ✜

8 Mussolini in Government

ひ෮ঌ৩

On June 15, 1921, Benito Mussolini took his place as a parliament deputy. He quickly caused trouble. He had strongly opposed the election of communist Francesco Misiano, who had won a seat in parliament. Now safe from arrest, Mussolini urged the other fascist deputies to physically remove Misiano from the parliament building. They followed Mussolini's order and dragged their fellow deputy through the hallway and down the stairs, spitting on him as they went. The Royal Guard, although charged with protecting the deputies, did nothing.

Other communist deputies angrily called for the fascist deputies to be thrown out of parliament. In a vote on the issue, the communists and socialists stood together. However, all the other deputies cast

Mussolini (front center) was one of many fascists who attended a political meeting in Rome in 1921.

their ballots in favor of the fascists. The majority also voted to kick Misiano out of office, shocking the communist and socialist deputies.

Mussolini did not stop there. In his first speech to parliament, he attacked socialism and suggested that Italians give up some personal freedoms and turn to a dictator. He said a dictator would bring order and prosperity back to Italy. Mussolini had planted the seed, and in time, he believed people would eventually see he was right.

In July, Giolitti resigned as prime minister and was replaced by Ivanhoe Bonomi. Among Bonomi's first acts as prime minister was to invite representatives of all political parties and trade unions to meet with parliament president Enrico De Nicola. De Nicola was charged with helping the groups reach a truce.

The meeting got off to a rocky start. The Catholic People's Party and the communists refused to send representatives. The socialists attended, as did the fascists, at Mussolini's urging.

The result of the gathering was the Treaty of Pacification. In the treaty, the groups vowed to end the violence toward one another. Mussolini stood among those who signed it. He realized that fascists needed to be seen as more than thugs if they were to gain respect among the Italian people and leaders around the world. Many fascists saw Mussolini's signing of the treaty as a betrayal. They ignored the treaty and continued committing violent acts against socialists.

In response, Mussolini agreed to step down as *Duce*—Italian for *leader*—and called a Fascist Party meeting on November 7, 1921. But it was all a show; he really had no intention of giving up his power. He prepared a speech in which he blamed the socialists for renewing the violence. Mussolini lied and said socialists had broken the treaty, while fascists were keeping the peace. The fascists liked what Mussolini had to say and chose to keep him as their *Duce*. By the end of 1921, membership in the Fascist Party exploded from 20,000 to nearly 250,000 in a year.

In February 1922, Luigi Facta became the sixth prime minister to try to turn the country around since the end of World War I four years earlier. However, he could do no more to help the Italian people than the prime ministers who had come before him.

Mussolini got ready to make his move. He tested Facta's power by planning assaults on governments in socialist cities. When Facta failed to respond to the attacks, Mussolini planned an assault

Luigi Facta (1861–1930)

on Rome. His goal was to overthrow the government and place himself as prime minister. But the assault on Rome would never happen. Without the support of the king, the Facta government crumbled. At first, the king tried to appease Mussolini and the Fascist Party by offering them several Cabinet positions. When Mussolini refused anything less than the position of prime minister, the king relented. At 39, Mussolini became the youngest prime minister in Italy's history. "Everything that is now wrong will be well," Mussolini told the Italian citizens after he took office.

Mussolini worked furiously, not to right the country, but to maintain his own newfound power. Among many service projects, he launched a massive effort to create 3,000 new farms and five agricultural towns in Rome. Mussolini often showed up at these projects with a small army of bodyguards, reporters, and photographers, making sure newspapers captured every good deed he did. He hoped people across the country would see these pictures and believe he really would make life better for them. "We shall succeed because we shall work," Mussolini said.

To the people of Italy, Mussolini appeared confident and strong. They were tired of suffering and hoped Mussolini would bring them peace and prosperity. Their new leader, however, was not truly interested in their happiness.

Mussolini made certain that his charity work was captured on camera and made known to the Italian people.

While he did not include any socialists or communists in his Cabinet, he did choose mostly nonfascists. This served two purposes. It did not allow any other fascists to become too powerful and rival him. It also kept the parties represented in Mussolini's Cabinet happy, believing they had a say in his government. Also, many of his Cabinet members were new to government. He did not want to choose people with many years of government experience. He believed an inexperienced Cabinet would fear him and be less likely to oppose his wishes.

On November 16, 1922, in his first speech to parliament, Mussolini shocked the fascists by saying

Mussolini was followed by members of his government after parliament appointed him prime minister.

he would not throw out the country's constitution. However, he threatened he might do so in the future if he deemed it necessary. The threat worked. Those who opposed Mussolini kept their mouths shut. They feared that if they spoke up, Mussolini would get rid of the constitution and create an entirely fascist government where they had no say.

In reality, the government Mussolini created was

just that. He asked that parliament grant him the powers of a dictator to get Italy back on track. Only the socialists and communists opposed his request, but they did not hold enough votes to block him. On November 27, armed with his "emergency" dictatorial powers, Mussolini adjourned parliament. Violence quickly developed against communists, socialists, and anyone else who might oppose him.

"I tell you that Italy is going ahead," Mussolini told a crowd in Florence seven months later. He told the excited citizens that he would be adding to Italy's territory. To do so, he worked to alter the Treaty of Versailles, which had ended World War I. He believed the Treaty of Versailles robbed Italy of the territory it had been promised when it joined the war.

On August 27, Mussolini had an excuse to go after some of that territory. A general and four other Italians were murdered that day on the border between Greece and Albania. The Italians killed were part of a group sent to settle a border dispute. Though the Greek government insisted the murderers were Albanian, Mussolini blamed the Greeks. He ordered the Greek government to apologize for the incident, pay a huge fine, and capture the murderers within five days and execute them.

The Greeks objected to Mussolini's demands. They said a trial judge would determine the criminals' fates, and the fine Mussolini asked for was too large.

They suggested the issue of the fine be brought to the League of Nations to determine a fair settlement. Mussolini responded by ordering 17 warships to Corfu, Greece. The leader of Corfu was warned that Italian forces would be taking over the island and that the flag must be lowered. When the order was ignored, Italian soldiers began firing on Corfu's citadel, which not only housed soldiers, but many civilians and children from two orphanages.

The world anxiously watched developments in Corfu. British officials feared Mussolini might start another war. Though they were not worried about their ability to defeat Mussolini, the British feared that if Mussolini's government fell, a communist government might replace it. This fear overrode the concern that Mussolini might try to expand his empire even farther. With no help coming from the League of Nations, Greece met all of Mussolini's demands. Satisfied, Mussolini pulled his forces out of Corfu.

The League of Nations formed in January 1920 as an international association of countries wanting to maintain peace after World War I. However, it proved ineffective in heading off World War II. Headquartered in Geneva, Switzerland, the League of Nations disbanded in 1946, about a year after the end of World War II, and was replaced by the United Nations.

The incident increased Mussolini's popularity in his homeland. It proved he was a man of action who was capable of leading Italy to victory. The League of Nations'

The presence of Italian soldiers in Corfu persuaded Greece to meet Mussolini's demands.

inaction in Corfu allowed Mussolini to bully other nations into giving in to his demands. In January 1924, Yugoslavia gave the town of Fiume to Italy without a fight. The Greeks also allowed Italy to occupy the Dodecanese Islands.

With his popularity soaring, Mussolini enacted a new law in the 1924 general election. Under the new law, for each majority party member elected, another member of the same party would also gain a seat. Knowing his own popularity and the fascists' ability to scare off opposing voters, Mussolini had no doubt that the fascists would become the majority party.

When the votes were counted after the April 1924 election, the fascists held 260 seats. Another 116 seats went to parties friendly to the fascists. The communists and socialists only managed to win 66 seats, and the Catholic People's Party earned 40.

One man dared to speak out against the election. Socialist deputy Giacomo Matteotti demanded the results be thrown out. Above the shouts of fascists who tried to drown him out, Matteotti talked about the Cheka, a secret police force that not only guarded Mussolini, but used fear and violence to silence the

Giacomo Matteotti (center) risked his life to have his voice heard.

opposition. Matteotti realized that by speaking out he would likely lose his life. However, he felt he could not quietly allow Mussolini to gain so much power. "You may kill me, but you will never kill my ideas," he said.

On June 10, 1924, Matteotti was beaten and kidnapped. A witness saw the car that whisked Matteotti away and jotted down the license plate number, but police did nothing with the information. After a member of Matteotti's family threatened to go to reporters with the information, a police official admitted the car belonged to a fascist newspaper editor. As a cover-up, Mussolini told his closest aides to spread the rumor that Matteotti had escaped to another country. Mussolini said, "If I get away with this we all survive, otherwise we shall all sink together."

Though Matteotti's death failed to bring down his regime, Mussolini was affected by the outcome. On June 12, he announced in parliament that no clues to Matteotti's whereabouts had been discovered. A deputy shouted out that Mussolini was involved in Matteotti's death. Other communists and socialists joined in voicing their accusations, which left Mussolini shaken.

Matteotti's battered body was found outside Rome in August, and those charged with his death said they believed it had been Mussolini's wish. Still, the prime minister remained popular with the people. ♋

9 MUSSOLINI, THE DICTATOR

‿◦〜◦‿

Through the years, Benito Mussolini continued to gain power. By 1930, all newspapers that opposed his views had disappeared. Mussolini created a law that allowed him to throw opposing members out of parliament and imprison without a trial anyone suspected of antifascist activity. The secret police could detain people as long as they wanted. He also created a law that forbade workers to strike. In time, the constitution and parliament became useless. All power lay in Mussolini's hands. Voicing opposition to him could prove deadly.

However, people were still willing to give up some of their personal freedoms in the hope that Mussolini would improve living conditions. Mussolini even gained the support of the Catholic Church. Officials

Mussolini would often become animated when trying to prove his point during a speech.

in the church believed Mussolini's rule was preferable to communist control. On February 11, 1929, the fascists and the Catholics signed the Lateran Treaty. Under the treaty, the Catholic Church recognized—for the first time in history—Italy and its power over all of Rome except for Vatican City. The church also agreed to stay out of politics. For his part, Mussolini agreed to declare the Roman Catholic faith the country's only state religion. He also recognized the independence of Vatican City.

Mussolini also worked to overhaul the school system. In December 1925, he ordered that schools "be inspired by the ideals of Fascism." Students of all ages learned fascist slogans. They also studied history and other classes that now carried a fascist slant. In addition, most children participated in after-school fascist youth activities. Boys as young as 4 underwent military training and learned about the Fascist Party. By the age of 8, boys performed drills with nonfiring miniatures of the Italian army's rifles.

Mussolini portrayed himself as a charming, loving family man as well as a steely dictator. By 1929,

With a population of about 1,000, Vatican City is the smallest independent nation in the world, but its influence stretches around the globe. Ruled by the pope, Vatican City is the spiritual and governmental center of the Roman Catholic Church. Surrounded by the city of Rome, Vatican City is made up of just 109 acres (43.6 hectares), the size of an average city park.

Young Italian boys marched in a fascist youth parade.

he and Rachele had five children and were living in a beautiful home. The family lived comfortably but modestly. Although he showed affection toward Edda, his oldest child, he did not have close relationships with the others. He also continued to cheat on his wife. In the fall of 1933, Mussolini would start an affair with Claretta Petacci that would continue for the rest of his life.

Mussolini distanced himself from most people in

Mussolini with his wife, Rachele, and his five children

his life. He never really had any close friends. He did not trust anyone, and he even developed a Roman salute to replace the handshake because he did not like to touch most people. Mussolini said:

> *A leader can have no equals, no friends,*
> *and must give his confidence to no one.*

Other world leaders watched Mussolini closely.

Among them was Adolf Hitler, who had been named Germany's chancellor in January 1933. Hitler and Mussolini met for the first time in June 1934 in Venice. Though they did not reach any agreements during their meetings, they talked about expansion plans. Both believed that adding territory to their countries was important. Among the nations Mussolini set his sights on was Ethiopia.

Italy had fought with Ethiopia regarding land issues in the late 1800s. However, by the time Mussolini came to power, the relationship between the two countries had grown relatively friendly. In the mid-1930s, Mussolini decided to change that. He wanted revenge for the Ethiopians defeating the Italians in 1896.

Mussolini said Ethiopians had attacked an Italian crew sent to survey the borders separating Ethiopia, Italian Somaliland, and British Somaliland. The Ethiopians denied any such attack and asked the League of Nations to settle the dispute, but Mussolini did not like the idea. Instead, he demanded the

Located in eastern Africa, Ethiopia is one of the world's oldest countries. It drew the world's attention in the 1970s and 1980s, when severe droughts led to widespread starvation throughout the impoverished nation. At the same time, Ethiopia was plagued with political unrest. Despite its world image as a desert wasteland, Ethiopia is a rugged, mountainous country that boasts some of the most beautiful views in the world. While drought is a continuing problem, it is mostly confined to the country's northernmost regions.

Ethiopians apologize for the incident and punish the people accused of starting the fight. To show his seriousness, he sent Italian troops to Ethiopia in February 1935.

Mussolini's military strength worked to keep other countries from getting involved in the dispute. However, the League of Nations did enact sanctions against Italy by banning the importation of Italian goods by member countries. It also forbade its members to sell products to Italy, including war materials. Still, Mussolini refused to back down. He demanded that he wanted half of Ethiopia's territory and that the Ethiopian army be disbanded.

Italians troops advanced into Ethiopia in early 1936.

When Ethiopia refused, war broke out. Appealing to his people's pride in a radio address about the war, Mussolini said:

> *Here is not just an army marching toward a military objective, but a whole nation, 44 million souls, against whom the blackest injustice has been committed: that of denying them a place in the sun.*

The Ethiopian army was no match for the Italians. Mussolini's military bombed hospitals and used deadly gas against Ethiopian troops and citizens alike. On May 5, 1936, Addis Ababa, the capital of Ethiopia, fell. The next month, Ethiopian leader Haile Selassie asked the League of Nations for help:

> *I ask the fifty-two nations, who have given the Ethiopian people a promise to help them in their resistance to the aggressor, what are they willing to do for Ethiopia? ... I ask what measures do you intend to take? ... What reply shall I have to take back to my people?"*

Haile Selassie came to power as Ethiopia's emperor in 1930. He claimed to be a descendant of King Solomon and the Queen of Sheba. When Italy overran Ethiopia in 1935, Selassie lived in exile in England. Once the British liberated Ethiopia in 1941, Selassie returned to power. He remained Ethiopia's emperor until 1974, when he was overthrown by military leaders.

At that point, members of the League of Nations realized they were too late to act. This showed Italy and other nations, including Germany and Japan, that they likely could overtake other nations and the world would not stop them.

Hitler quickly made use of this knowledge. In March 1936, he broke the Treaty of Versailles by marching troops into the Rhineland, a safety zone between France and Germany. According to the treaty, German troops were forbidden to enter the Rhineland. Later that year, both Hitler and Mussolini sent aid to General Francisco Franco in his bid to take over Spain's government. The Spanish Civil War provided Italy and Germany the opportunity to practice warfare. In particular, Italy and Germany used the fight in Spain to give their air forces practice bombing civilian targets. By the time Franco and his fascists took control of Spain in 1939, Hitler and Mussolini had become close allies.

While civil war raged in Spain, Hitler focused on securing more territory for his growing empire. In September 1938, he greedily eyed a mostly German part of Czechoslovakia known as Sudetenland. British Prime Minister Neville Chamberlain helped work out a deal in which Germany would annex Sudetenland. For his part, Hitler promised he would now be satisfied and cease Germany's expansion. Though Czechoslovakian leaders were expected to live with the compromise, they were not allowed to take part in the negotiations. With the deal worked out, Chamberlain believed he had helped the world avoid another war and returned to Great Britain relieved and triumphant. Chamberlain told his citizens:

> *My good friends ... this is the second time in our history that there has come back from Germany to Downing Street peace with honor. I believe it is peace for our time. I thank you from the bottom of our hearts. And now I recommend you go home and sleep quietly in your beds."*

Neville Chamberlain (left) tried to appease Adolf Hitler by giving Germany control of more land.

However, Hitler had no intention of honoring the agreement Chamberlain had helped design. On March 15, 1939, German troops invaded the rest of Czechoslovakia while the world looked on. Following Hitler's example, Italy invaded Albania on April 7, gaining control of the country in less than a week.

On May 22, Hitler and Mussolini signed what the Italian dictator called The Pact of Steel, an agreement that made Italy and Germany full-scale military allies. If either country started a war, the other promised to help. In reality, Italy had little to offer. Its army only numbered 160,000 men, not the 2 million Mussolini

Mussolini (left) and Hitler rode together in a procession in Munich, Germany.

had first boasted. In addition, its military equipment was outdated. Mussolini quickly realized his mistake and sent word to Hitler that Italy would not be ready for a large-scale war for another four to eight years. Hitler, however, said he would not be delayed and expected help from the Italians if needed.

However, Hitler quickly proved he did not need Italy for his immediate plans. In August 1939, Germany signed a nonaggression agreement with Russia. Russian dictator Joseph Stalin promised not to go to war if Germany attacked neighboring Poland. In return, Hitler promised to split Poland with Russia. Italy played no part in the agreement, which angered Mussolini. He did not like feeling unimportant to Hitler. Yet Mussolini kept quiet, perhaps out of fear of Hitler.

In September 1939, the German army tore through Poland. Mussolini did his best to keep out of the fight, saying he believed Germany could easily handle the situation on its own. However, others were honoring their promises. Both France and Great Britain had vowed to come to Poland's aid if Germany attacked. When Poland was invaded, France and Great Britain declared war on Germany. World War II had begun. ✎

Chapter
10 WAR AND DEATH

❧⟨✦⟩❧

In 1940, the new British prime minister, Winston Churchill, tried to mend his nation's relationship with Mussolini. He hoped this would keep Italy from joining Germany in the fight in Europe.

Great Britain could prove to be a big threat to Italy. It controlled both Gibraltar and the Suez Canal, blocking Italy in the Mediterranean, its only sea route. Yet Mussolini refused to ally his country with the British. Great Britain honored its promise to come to Poland's aid after it was attacked by Germany; Italy would honor its pact with Germany. On June 10, Italy declared war on France and Great Britain. It was less than two weeks before France would fall, and Italy shared in the spoils of war by helping Germany occupy France.

Dressed in military uniform, Mussolini addressed his troops during World War II.

Because his military was not very strong, Mussolini planned a mostly defensive war strategy. He did not really want to enter the fight, but when he saw Germany quickly winning Europe, he realized that Italy had better join the war soon or risk being left out of the spoils again. He only considered attacking those he saw as weaker nations.

On September 13, Italy mounted an attack against Egypt. The fighting went well for the Italians until December 9. On that day, a British force about one-fourth the size of the Italian army broke through a gap in the Italian line and pushed them out of Egypt.

The Italians fared no better against the Greeks. Though Italy attacked Greece in October 1940 and occupied a large portion of the country, the enemy proved stronger than expected. From November 22 to December 23, the Greeks went on the offensive and pushed the Italian soldiers back to the Adriatic Sea. When the Italians retreated to a naval base at Valona, the British bombed it. The Italians lost many soldiers and large quantities of war materials.

In early 1941, Italians suffered the war's effects on their own soil—the British began bombing Italy. In addition, news on other fronts grew worse. The Italian army had made progress against Great Britain in British Somaliland, but in January 1941, the Allies had turned the situation around. Great Britain invaded Ethiopia and Italian Somaliland, and

An Allied air raid destroyed a row of buildings in Italy.

on April 4, the Allies captured Addis Ababa. The next month, Haile Selassie was returned to his throne. Italy would lose all its colonies to the British.

Mussolini worked hard to make his people believe these defeats were victories—or to at least downplay the seriousness of the losses. He promised his citizens that in time, Great Britain would be defeated. Mussolini placed any blame for failure on his generals. In time, he would turn on the Italian people themselves. He would say Italians were weak and cowardly.

Mussolini's harsh comments made Italian people

angry. They were frustrated with losing loved ones in a war Italy was losing. They grew weary of being bombed and of the destruction it caused. Day-to-day living became more and more difficult. Italy was hit with severe food shortages, and many went to bed hungry every night.

On June 22, 1941, Hitler attacked Russia, turning on his former ally. Mussolini sent Italian troops to aid the Germans, who seemed to be pushing into Russia with ease. He hoped that joining what he believed would be a winning battle would make Italians happier and more hopeful. But the German progress in Russia did not last long. In November, aided by a harsh early winter, the Russian troops started pushing the Germans back.

As Germany faced defeat, Hitler expected Italy to help out in whatever ways he desired. About 350,000 Italians were sent to work in German war plants and were treated like slaves. Anger grew in Italy as family and friends learned about the horrible conditions their loved ones faced in Germany.

In June 1942, the Italian navy scored victories in the Mediterranean Sea by sinking British ships. Mussolini enjoyed a view of the battle from an Italian airplane. He also traveled to North Africa to lift the spirits of Italian troops fighting there against the British.

When Mussolini returned to Italy, he fell ill with

stomach problems he had suffered during his adult life. While he was sick, the Allies crept closer to Italy. After clearing the Axis forces—as Italy, Germany, and Japan were known—out of North Africa, the Allies attacked a fortress between Tunisia and Sicily. After about a week of fighting, the fortress fell.

The Axis powers controlled much of Europe in 1942.

By now, even many of those closest to Mussolini were begging him to surrender, but he refused. As his people starved and suffered more losses, Mussolini continued the fight.

In July 1943, British and American forces landed in Sicily. Twenty years before, Mussolini had cracked down on the Sicilian Mafia, or organized criminals. Now, they helped the Allies by serving as guides through the mountains and clearing the roads of snipers. By August 17, the Allies controlled Sicily, a prime place from which to launch an invasion of mainland Italy. "They are knocking at the gate," Mussolini said of the Allies.

He had no plan for defending his nation. Realizing this, even those who had remained loyal to Mussolini began to turn on him. Knowing he needed help, he went to Hitler. With no other choices remaining, Mussolini listened quietly as Hitler suggested that Italian troops be reorganized under a German commander.

While Mussolini met with Hitler, Rome and other large cities in Italy were bombed by the Allies. Fascist leaders believed something had to be done. They decided to remove Mussolini as commander in chief and gave control of the military to the king. The parliament and constitution were brought back, but Mussolini did nothing. He knew he had lost the support of his party and of most Italians.

On July 25, Mussolini met with the king, who told him:

An Italian newspaper headline pronounced "Long Live Free Italy" after the king took control of the military.

> *My dear Duce, it's no longer any good. Italy has gone to bits. Army morale is at rock bottom. The soldiers don't want to fight any more. You can certainly be under no illusions as to Italy's feeling with regard to yourself. At this moment you are the most hated man in Italy.*

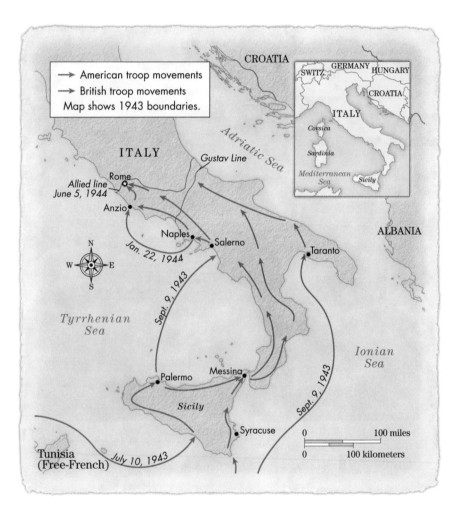

American troop movements
British troop movements
Map shows 1943 boundaries.

CROATIA

GERMANY HUNGARY
SWITZ.
CROATIA
ITALY
Corsica
Sardinia
Mediterranean Sea
Sicily

ITALY

Adriatic Sea

Gustav Line

Rome
Allied line June 5, 1944
Anzio

Naples
Jan. 22, 1944
Salerno

Sept. 9, 1943

Taranto

ALBANIA

Tyrrhenian Sea

N W E S

Ionian Sea

Palermo
Messina
Sicily
Sept. 9, 1943
Syracuse

Tunisia (Free-French)
July 10, 1943

0   100 miles
0   100 kilometers

The Invasion of Sicily marked the end of Mussolini's rule of Italy.

After a 20-minute discussion, Mussolini agreed to step down. His reign had ended. "I challenged the world and it proved too strong for me; I despised other men and they are taking their revenge," he said.

Mussolini was arrested and imprisoned to protect him from those who might do him harm. On August 28, he was moved to an abandoned hotel in the mountains north of Rome.

On September 8, Italy's new prime minister, Pietro Badoglio, announced that he had made peace with the Allies. However, Germany's Hitler was not ready to give up. He made plans to put Mussolini back in power. According to Mussolini, a glider landed about 100 yards (91 meters) from the hotel where he was being held. Four or five men climbed out of the glider, set up machine guns, and moved toward the hotel. Other gliders landed and followed the same routine. Among the Germans was an Italian officer, and Mussolini yelled to his guards not to shoot him. The guards lowered their guns, and Mussolini was taken to a waiting German airplane without a fight.

"I knew all along that the Führer [Hitler] would give me this proof of his friendship," Mussolini said.

After his escape, Mussolini became Hitler's puppet, doing whatever the German dictator ordered him to do. His first task was a radio address in which he told the Italian people that the king and the new Italian prime minister had betrayed Italy. Mussolini promised that with the help of the Germans, he had led Italy to victory despite the prime minister's surrender.

Hitler set up Mussolini's government in northern Italy. Mussolini wanted to return to Rome, but Hitler did not want him there because the Germans were in control of Rome. Hitler did not want Mussolini causing any problems in that city. Not daring to argue,

Mussolini stayed in northern Italy and created his own government. Hitler let him do what he wanted as long as Mussolini did not interfere with any of his plans.

Mussolini decided to capture those who had betrayed him, including his daughter Edda's husband, Count Galeazzo Ciano. When fascist leaders had voted to remove Mussolini as commander in chief, Ciano had agreed with them. He believed that a new

Mussolini's daughter Edda with her husband, Count Ciano

prime minister would have a place for him in the new government, but he was wrong. Mussolini charged his son-in-law with treason. Despite Edda's pleas for mercy, Mussolini had her husband executed on January 11, 1944.

But Mussolini's days were numbered as well. On June 5, Rome fell into Allied hands. Unable to eat or sleep, Mussolini was near mental collapse. With an Allied victory assured, Mussolini thought about escaping from Italy. But where could he go? No one wanted him, including his fellow Italians.

Though his German guards told him not to go to Milan, Mussolini ignored their advice. On April 25, 1945, Mussolini fled in a car with a friend without any resistance from the Germans. Two days later, Mussolini and his friend joined a group of about 200 German soldiers heading to Switzerland. However, the group was stopped before it reached the border. The Italian commander who stopped them said he would let the German soldiers continue their journey, but first he wanted to make sure no Italians had joined their group. Disguised only with a German helmet, Mussolini was easy to spot. Mussolini and other Italians were taken to the northern Italian village of Dongo.

Mussolini's mistress, Claretta Petacci, had planned to meet him on his way to Switzerland. However, she too had been caught and sent to Dongo. Reunited with Mussolini, Petacci refused to leave his side. Mussolini and Petacci were put in a guarded farmhouse.

Mussolini knew he didn't have long to live, and his thoughts were of his wife, Rachele. The last letter he ever wrote was to Rachele as he awaited his fate. "On my knees I ask you to forgive me all the evil I have unwillingly done you; but you know that you are the one woman whose good I genuinely desired," he wrote.

*Claretta Petacci
(1912–1945)*

Mussolini was sentenced to die. He and Petacci were taken outside the farmhouse. Mussolini's death sentence was read aloud, and two gunmen were ordered to fire. Petacci died instantly, but Mussolini was only wounded by the first shot when the gun jammed. A second shot from a different gun ended his life.

The bodies of Mussolini and Petacci were loaded into the back of a truck and transported to Milan. They were hung upside down in the town square as a public spectacle. The dead bodies of 12 other Italian leaders hung next to them for all to mock and scorn

for what they had done to Italy and its citizens.

The Allies went on to win World War II, but it would take time for Italy to recover from the ravages of war. Among its first steps was to choose a new form of government. In a 1946 vote, Italians chose to establish a republic led by a president and abolish the monarchy, or rule by a king. In 1947, Italy approved a new constitution, which detailed the new system of government. Mussolini's dreams of a dictatorship for Italy were forever buried with him. ✍

Vittorio Mussolini visited the tomb of his father at San Cassino cemetery in Predappio, Italy.

MUSSOLINI'S LIFE

1883

Born July 29 in
Verano di Costa,
Italy

1892

Sent to boarding
school in Faenza

1893

Is expelled
from Faenza
school and sent
to school in
Forlimpopoli

1880

1895

1886

Grover Cleveland
dedicates the Statue
of Liberty in New York
Harbor, a gift from the
people of France

1893

Women gain
voting privileges
in New Zealand,
the first country to
take such a step

WORLD EVENTS

1905

Begins mandatory 21 months of military service in Italy in January

1902

Teaches in Gualtieri but contract is not renewed in June; travels to Switzerland

1901

Graduates from Forlimpopoli with a teaching certificate

1900

1905

1898

The Spanish-American War gains Cuba its independence; Spain cedes the Phillipines, Guam, and Puerto Rico to the United States for $20 million

1903

Brothers Orville and Wilbur Wright successfully fly a powered airplane

MUSSOLINI'S LIFE

1909

Moves to Trent, Italy, to edit weekly socialist newspaper; fathers a child with Fernanda Oss Facchinelli, but the child soon dies

1908

Teaches for four months on the Italian Riviera

1906

Takes job as teacher in Tolmezzo

1906

Earthquake and fires destroy most of San Francisco; more than 3,000 people die

1909

The National Association for the Advancement of Colored People (NAACP) is founded

WORLD EVENTS

1910

Begins living with Rachele Guidi in Forli in January; daughter Edda is born in September

1912

Chosen as editor of *Avanti!* in November and moves to Milan

1914

Resigns from *Avanti!* in October and starts his own newspaper in November

1910

1912

The *Titanic* sinks on its maiden voyage; more than 1,500 people die

1914

Archduke Franz Ferdinand is assassinated, launching World War I (1914–1918)

MUSSOLINI'S LIFE

1922

Becomes prime minister on October 29

1915

Drafted into the army August 31; marries Rachele December 16

1921

Elected to parliament

1920

1917

Vladimir Lenin and Leon Trotsky lead Bolsheviks in a rebellion against the Russian government during the October Revolution

1923

Irish Civil War ends and the rebels sign a peace treaty

WORLD EVENTS

1943

Resigns as
prime minister
July 25

1945

Executed
April 28

1939

Signs The Pact
of Steel with
Hitler May 22

1940

1939

German troops
invade Poland;
Britain and
France declare
war on Germany;
World War II
(1939–1945) begins

1944

Operation Overlord
begins on D-Day
with the land-
ing of 155,000
Allied troops on
the beaches of
Normandy, France

1945

World War II
(1939–1945) ends

DATE OF BIRTH: July 29, 1883

BIRTHPLACE: Verano di Costa, Italy

FATHER: Alessandro Mussolini (?–1910)

MOTHER: Rosa Mussolini (?–1905)

EDUCATION: Graduated from Forlimpopoli school in 1901 with a teaching certificate

SPOUSE: Rachele Guidi (1890–1979)

DATE OF MARRIAGE: December 16, 1915

CHILDREN: Edda (1910–1995)
Vittorio (1916–1997)
Bruno (1918–1941)
Romano (1927–2006)
Anna-Maria (1929–)

OTHER CHILDREN: Benito Albino (1915–?) (with Ida Dalser)

DATE OF DEATH: April 28, 1945

PLACE OF BURIAL: Family mausoleum in the San Cassiano cemetery

FURTHER READING

Ambrose, Stephen E. *The Good Fight: How World War II Was Won.* New York: Atheneum Books for Young Readers, 2001.

Mulvihill, Margaret. *Mussolini and Italian Fascism.* New York: Franklin Watts, 1990.

Pavlovic, Zoran. *Italy.* Philadelphia: Chelsea House, 2004.

Roberts, Jeremy. *Benito Mussolini.* Minneapolis: Twenty-First Century Books, 2006.

LOOK FOR MORE SIGNATURE LIVES BOOKS ABOUT THIS ERA:

Benazir Bhutto: *Pakistani Prime Minister and Activist*

Fidel Castro: *Leader of Communist Cuba*

Madame Chiang Kai-shek: *Face of Modern China*

Winston Churchill: *British Soldier, Writer, Statesman*

Indira Gandhi: *Political Leader in India*

Jane Goodall: *Legendary Zoologist*

Adolf Hitler: *Dictator of Nazi Germany*

Queen Noor: *American-Born Queen of Jordan*

Eva Peron: *First Lady of Argentina*

Joseph Stalin: *Dictator of the Soviet Union*

ON THE WEB

For more information on this topic,
use FactHound.

1. Go to *www.facthound.com*
2. Type in this book ID: 075651892X
3. Click on the *Fetch It* button.

FactHound will find the best
Web sites for you.

HISTORIC SITES

Eldred World War II Museum
201 Main St.
Eldred, PA 16731
814/225-2220
Museum about World War II with artifacts
from the era

War Eagles Air Museum
8012 Airport Road
Santa Teresa, NM 88008
505/589-2000
Museum about aircraft used during World
War II and the Korean conflict

alimony
money given to the spouse after a couple has divorced

amnesty
the act of an authority or government by which pardon is granted to a large group of individuals

assassination
the murder of someone who is well known or important, often for political reasons

asylum
hospital for people who are mentally ill

coalition
alliance of people or groups working toward a common goal

communism
a system in which goods and property are owned by the government and shared in common

dictator
a ruler who takes complete control of a country, often unjustly

fascist
person who believes in a form of government that promotes extreme nationalism, repression, anti-communism, and is ruled by a dictator

frugally
not wasting resources

libel
a lie that is intentionally printed

mausoleum
building that houses tombs

oppression
an unjust or cruel exercise of authority or power

politics
the debate and activity involved in governing
a country

revolutionary
to bring about a major change

scabs
people who take the job of workers when they
are on strike

socialist
follower of an economic system in which the government owns most businesses

strike
a work stoppage by employees as a protest
against an employer

terrorism
the systematic use of violent or destructive acts as
a way to control other people

tyranny
government in which all the power is in the hands
of one ruler, who keeps people in their place by
using threats

Chapter 2

Page 18, line 6: Alan Axelrod. *The Life and Work of Benito Mussolini.* Indianapolis: Alpha Books, 2002, p. 10.

Page 18, line 18: Margherita G. Sarfatti. *The Life of Benito Mussolini.* New York: Frederick A. Stokes Company, 1925, p. 31.

Chapter 4

Page 34, line 19: *The Life and Work of Benito Mussolini,* p. 49.

Chapter 6

Page 48, line 15: Ibid., p. 81.

Chapter 8

Page 62, line 10: Henry Adams and the editors of Time-Life books. *Italy at War.* Alexandria, Va: Time-Life Books, 1982, p. 11.

Page 62, line 22: Ibid.

Page 65, line 9: Benito Mussolini. *Mussolini: As Revealed in His Political Speeches.* New York: Howard Fertig, 1976, p. 329.

Page 69, line 3: *The Life and Work of Benito Mussolini,* p. 168.

Page 69, line 14: Denis Mack Smith. *Mussolini.* New York: Alfred A. Knopf, 1982, p. 78.

Chapter 9

Page 72, line 13: *The Life and Work of Benito Mussolini,* p. 196.

Page 74, line 5: *Mussolini,* p. 110.

Page 77, line 4: *Italy at War,* p. 31.

Page 77, line 17: *The Life and Work of Benito Mussolini,* p. 221.

Page 79, line 6: Ibid., p. 249.

Chapter 10

Page 88, line 12: *Italy at War,* p. 143.

Page 89, line 3: Ibid., p. 156.

Page 90, line 2: *Mussolini,* p. 317.

Page 91, line 15: *The Life and Work of Benito Mussolini,* p. 293.

Page 94, line 12: Roman Dombrowski. *Mussolini: Twilight and Fall.* Wesport, Conn.: Hyperion Press, Inc., 1979, p. 178.

Adams, Henry, and the editors of Time-Life Books. *Italy at War*. Alexandria, Va.: Time-Life Books, 1982.

Axelrod, Alan. *The Life and Work of Benito Mussolini*. Indianapolis: Alpha Books, 2002.

Collier, Richard. *Duce! A Biography of Benito Mussolini*. New York: Viking Press, 1971.

Dombrowski, Roman. *Mussolini: Twilight and Fall*. Westport, Conn.: Hyperion Press, Inc., 1979.

Mussolini, Benito. *Benito Mussolini: Memoirs 1942–1943*. New York: Howard Fertig, 1975.

Mussolini, Benito. *Mussolini: As Revealed in His Political Speeches*. New York: Howard Fertig, 1976.

Sarfatti, Margherita G. *The Life of Benito Mussolini*. New York: Frederick A. Stokes Company, 1925.

Smith, Denis Mack. *Mussolini*. New York: Alfred A. Knopf, 1982.

Brenda Haugen started in the newspaper business and had a career as an award-winning journalist before finding her niche as an author. Since then, she has written and edited many books, most of them for children. A graduate of the University of North Dakota in Grand Forks, Brenda lives in North Dakota with her family.

Image Credits